Getting Around

Please visit our web site at: www.garethstevens.com
For a free color catalog describing Gareth Stevens'
list of high-quality books and multimedia programs,
call 1-800-542-2595 (USA) or 1-800-461-9120 (Canada).
Gareth Stevens Publishing's Fax: (414) 332-3567.

Library of Congress Cataloging-in-Publication Data available upon request from publisher. Fax: (414) 336-0157 for the attention of the Publishing Records Department.

ISBN 0-8368-2816-X

This North American edition first published in 2001 by
Gareth Stevens Publishing
330 West Olive Street, Suite 100
Milwaukee, WI 53212 USA

© QA International, 2000

Created and produced as *So Many Ways to Move About* by

QA INTERNATIONAL
329, rue de la Commune Ouest, 3ᵉ étage
Montréal, Québec
Canada H2Y 2E1
Tel.: (514) 499-3000 Fax: (514) 499-3010
www.qa-international.com

Printed in Canada

1 2 3 4 5 6 7 8 9 05 04 03 02 01

Gareth Stevens Publishing
A WORLD ALMANAC EDUCATION GROUP COMPANY

Getting from place to place

Most living beings can move from one place to another. They use their legs, wings, fins, flippers, or tails. They swim, fly, climb, and move around above and below the ground in groups or by themselves. Animals move for many reasons: to escape harm, to find food, to find mates, or to find a place to live.

A river mammal

A large hippopotamus might weigh close to 3,000 pounds (1,361 kilograms). This African mammal spends most of its time in rivers. It uses its webbed feet to swim so fast that it appears to be flying through the water. A hippopotamus can also walk underwater along the bottom of a riverbed.

hippopotamus

An expert hoverer

This tiny bird is only about 4 inches (10 centimeters) long. The hummingbird can fly as fast as 25 miles (40 kilometers) per hour. It can also beat its wings more than 50 times a second and can hover in the air for as long as four hours at a time!

rufous hummingbird

eastern grey kangaroo

Living life by leaps and bounds

The eastern grey kangaroo lives in Australia. It grows to about 6.5 feet (2 meters) tall. A kangaroo can move as fast as 31 miles (50 km) per hour. It does this by taking great leaps — as far as 30 feet (9 m). To leap, the kangaroo uses its powerful hind legs and balances itself with its long tail.

A fish out of water

Not all fish live in water! This mudskipper lives in mangrove swamps. It moves by using its tail and fins to skip along on top of the mud. It has no lungs, so it breathes by taking in oxygen through its skin.

3

mudskipper

Are you curious?

A young hippopotamus learns how to swim before it can walk. Special valves keep its nostrils and ears closed when it is underwater. It can hold its breath for almost two minutes. When it needs a rest, it climbs onto its mother's back.

Animals that swim

Water is much more dense than air. To move around in water, animals must have special tools. Many animals that swim have fins and streamlined bodies that help them move through the water with ease. Fins also help these swimmers steer and keep their balance as they speed through the water. Although fish are the best swimmers, some reptiles, birds, and mammals spend their lives in water, too.

A mammal in a diving suit

Dolphins are among the best swimmers in the oceans and seas. Their skin is smooth and rubbery. Dolphins have sleek bodies and powerful muscles. They have a fin on their backs and fins on their tails. The tail fins are called flukes. Dolphins move their flukes up and down to swim. They can go as fast as 40 miles (64 km) per hour.

Atlantic spotted dolphin

mackerel shark

Swift and powerful

The fierce mackerel shark makes its home in the Atlantic Ocean. It can reach speeds as fast as 37 miles (60 km) per hour! This powerful shark hunts down schools of mackerel and herring, and it can swallow a swordfish without even slowing down. This huge fish is almost 13 feet (4 m) long and can leap up to 23 feet (7 m) in the air!

Swimming speed record

The swordfish is an excellent swimmer. Its body is as streamlined as a jet airplane, and it can swim as fast as 68 miles (110 km) per hour. This fish can chase schools of herring and mackerel over great distances. It also leaps high above the water and can grow to 19 feet (6 m) long.

swordfish

A turtle with a leathery shell

At over 8 feet (2.5 m) long, the leatherback turtle is the largest turtle alive. Its webbed front feet are very broad and strong. They allow the turtle to move 328 feet (100 m) in barely 10 seconds! This reptile has a bony shell that is covered with smooth, leathery skin. Its skin allows the turtle to glide through the water easily.

leatherback turtle

Are you curious?

In the middle of the twentieth century, scientists designed a special rubber covering for submarines. It was modeled on the skin of the dolphin. This "diving suit" greatly improved the performance of submarines.

Swimmers without fins

Not all water animals have fins, but they can still get around. Snakes, eels, and leeches move up and down in a wavy motion, called undulating. Squid move forward by releasing jets of water behind them. Penguins swim by using their wings as fins. On the surface of the water, insects use their feet as oars and waterbirds row with their webbed feet.

Underwater movement

The nautilus has a spiral shell that is divided into about 30 small chambers, or sections. The chambers are filled with air and liquid. A siphon passes through each chamber. The siphon can pump water in and out of the chambers, allowing the nautilus to rise up, sink down, or move forward.

pearly nautilus

Strange birds

Adélie penguins cannot fly, so they throw themselves into the icy Antarctic waters. To swim, they use their wings and webbed feet. On land, they sometimes move around by sliding along the ice on their bellies, using their feet and wings to pull themselves forward.

Adélie penguin

sea snake

Underwater undulations

On solid ground, the sea snake moves with great skill. Underwater, it swims like a champion. Using its tail, it paddles and undulates through the water in search of prey. This reptile has dangerous venom that can poison human beings.

Arctic loon

Remarkable divers

7

Ducks and loons have large webbed feet, which they use as oars. A special gland at the base of their backs produces an oil that makes their feathers waterproof. The Arctic loon is an excellent swimmer and diver. It can dive as deep as 230 feet (70 m) and stay underwater for as long as five minutes.

Are you curious?

Mollusks are related to octopuses and cuttlefish, but they are the only cephalopods that have a shell for a home. Their bodies are in the first chamber of their shells.

Expert walkers

Some walkers move over solid ground. Some walk on the surface of the water or on the ocean floor. Each walker has a special style and a special set of equipment. Birds and human beings walk on two feet. Insects wander around on six legs. Crustaceans stroll across the ocean floor on eight legs. Starfish crawl on a thousand little tube feet. Centipedes pace up and down on hundreds of legs.

Walking on water lilies

The jaçana walks across the surface of the water on lotuses, water lilies, and other floating plants. Its long toes are like snowshoes. They support the bird's body weight to keep it from sinking. This bird's feet are perfect for walking on water, but it has trouble moving on land.

African jaçana

8

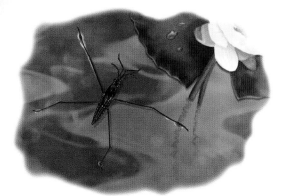

water strider

Insect on skates

With each step, a water strider glides gracefully across the surface of the water. Its short front legs capture prey. Its middle legs row to move the insect forward. Its hind legs serve as a rudder. A clump of hairs under its body traps air and keeps the insect from getting wet!

giant crab

The great sea walker

The giant crab has long legs so it can move around on the floors of the deepest oceans. This crab is the largest crustacean in the world. Its body measures 12 inches (30 cm) in diameter. When fully extended, its legs span a little over 10 feet (3 m)!

Feet, feet, and more feet...

Millipedes do not actually have 1,000 feet. Most of them have fewer than 200! As julids slowly snake their way through damp soil and rotting vegetation, they move all the legs on one side of their body almost at the same time. This way of walking makes a wavelike motion that passes through the entire length of the insect's body.

julid

Are you curious?

The nest of the jaçana is very simple. It is made from reeds, leaves, and the stems of water lilies. The nest rests on floating plants. The jaçana's eggs have a coating that protects them from the water.

Excellent acrobats

Squirrels and monkeys leap from branch to branch. They perform many acrobatic feats and high-flying stunts. Woodpeckers, tree creepers, dormice, and martens climb tree trunks with great skill. Flies and lizards move around on ceilings with ease. These excellent acrobats are well equipped to perform their feats. Many of them have light, supple bodies or powerful legs and claws. Some have prehensile tails that they can use as a fifth limb when needed.

A ceiling walker

The tokay gecko can grow to be 14 inches (35 cm) long. This large lizard can climb up and down walls. It can even walk on ceilings! How does it do this? Under each toe are thousands of bristles that act like suckers and allow the lizard to cling to almost any smooth surface.

Are you curious?

The tokay gecko makes a sound like the bark of a dog. It likes to live with human beings. When people hear the lizard's cry, they believe it is a sign of happiness.

tokay gecko

A very practical limb

Some animals spend a lot of time in trees. Spider monkeys and opossums use their tails as if they were another arm or leg. The tail of a tree porcupine is strong enough to coil firmly around tree branches, so the porcupine can feed on leaves, stems, and fruit without falling.

A South American
prehensile-tailed porcupine

white-handed gibbon

The acrobat of tropical forests

Gibbons are ace acrobats. These small apes use their long, strong arms to swing from branch to branch as they travel through the tops of tropical trees to find food. They can leap through the air as much as 33 feet (10 m) at a time and reach speeds of nearly 20 miles (32 km) per hour!

A champion climber

The Eurasian nuthatch is a small bird that has long, strong toes with sturdy nails. The nails can sink into the bark of trees. When looking for food on a tree trunk, this bird can move in any direction. It can move upward. It can move downward — head first. It can also hop from side to side. These little birds sleep with their heads tucked into a crack in the bark of a tree!

Eurasian nuthatch

Flying aces

We often think of flying as just another way to get from one place to another. Birds, bats, and insects, however, are blessed with something special — wings. Some wings are short, some are long. Some are narrow, some wide. Some are designed for quick takeoffs, others for rapid flights. Some wings enable long flights, some are made for hovering. Some are used for gliding, some for fancy moves. The wings of flyers are perfectly adapted to the needs of each animal.

An expert glider

The wandering albatross uses air currents, whirlwinds, and strong gusts to swoop upward, downward, and in zigzag patterns over the Atlantic Ocean. It travels more than 60 miles (100 km) without flapping its wings even once! The albatross is one of the largest birds that are able to fly. Its long, narrow wings can span about 11 feet (3.5 m).

wandering albatross

Air moves

Dragonflies are slender and delicate. They are among the fastest of all insects. Powered by two pairs of rigid wings, these insects can reach speeds of 50 miles (80 km) per hour! A dragonfly can fly backward, hover in one place, or fly straight up, like a helicopter.

dragonfly

A tireless flier

No bird spends more time in the air than the common swift. It spends its day feeding, cleaning itself, reproducing, gathering nesting materials, and even sleeping — all high in the air! When it does take a rest, this small bird lands on a vertical surface and clings to it with the sturdy claws on its short legs.

common swift

13

Flying mammals

Bats are are the only mammals that can fly. Their wings are a thin membrane of skin that stretches from the shoulder and is supported by the arm, the forearm, and five very long fingers. These little acrobats can reach speeds of more than 30 miles (50 km) per hour.

spear-nosed bat

Are you curious?

Some sailors believe the albatross is a sign that bad weather is coming. Others believe the bird may be the reborn spirit of sailors lost at sea.

Leapers and gliders

Some species of animals leap and glide to move around in the air. A few have special membranes that act like little parachutes! These creatures cover amazing distances as they throw themselves into the air and travel from branch to branch.

Flying from tree to tree

The flying lemur is about the size of a cat. It has a membrane of skin that stretches from neck to tail on each side of its body. When all four legs are stretched out, that membrane acts like a parachute! The flying lemur can move from branch to branch without touching the ground. It can glide up to 100 yards (91 m)!

flying lemur

Traveling on a thread

The crab spider spins a long thread of silk. This thread is held up by warm air currents that may carry the spider a long way by the wind. When the temperature drops and the air becomes too cold, the spider must land. On the ground, it can walk backward and sideways, just like a crab.

red-spotted crab spider

flying dragon

A lizard with wings

Flying dragons are reptiles about 8 inches (20 cm) long. They live in the tops of tall trees, and they leap and glide through the air to search for food. Two large folds of skin attached to the sides of their bodies act like wings. Flying dragons can glide as far as 200 feet (61 m).

Flying like a fish

The hatchetfish is barely 2.5 inches (6 cm) long and lives in the rivers, swamps, and ditches of Central America. Its fins are strong muscles that allow it to leap above the water and glide. By flapping its fins like wings, this fish can travel above the water for several feet (meters)!

common hatchetfish

Are you curious?

The young flying lemur travels around on its mother's belly. When she wants to glide, the mother folds over part of her "parachute," creating a snug hammock for her little one.

Champion jumpers

What do fleas, grasshoppers, pumas, deer, giant kangaroos, weasels, and frogs have in common? They are all great jumpers, and they can cover very long distances in only seconds. These creatures jump for many reasons: to escape enemies, to hunt prey, or just to move around. Jumpers are much faster than walkers, and they get much less tired than runners. Their special muscles allow them to perform amazing feats.

A long-jump champion

The snow leopard creeps along a tree branch, using its long tail to keep its balance. From this high perch, it waits and watches for a meal. It is looking for a wild boar, a deer, a sheep, or maybe a goat. Suddenly, the powerful animal jumps. It can cover 50 feet (15 m) in a single bound! Its long, low body makes it the best jumper in the cat family.

snow leopard

The power of a giant

The killer whale is the largest and fastest member of the dolphin family. Its body is about 30 feet (9 m) long, and its dorsal fin is almost 7 feet (2 m) high. When this giant of the seas heaves its huge body out of the water, it can leap 33 feet (10 m) into the air! This talented animal stars in water shows.

killer whale

Field hopper

The great green bush-cricket is about 1.6 inches (4 cm) long. This insect is not a very good walker, runner, or flier. Its long, powerful legs are perfect for jumping, however. The great green bush-cricket can make leaps that measure 75 times its body length!

great green bush-cricket

desert jerboa

Jumping jerboas!

The desert jerboa lives in the deserts and dry areas of North Africa and the Middle East. This small rodent looks like a miniature kangaroo. It has a special way of escaping from its enemies. Its long hind legs help it jump like a spring. It can jump as far as 13 feet (4 m) and reach speeds of 15 miles (25 km) per hour!

Are you curious?

Although buying and selling snow-leopard fur is against the law in many countries, it still goes on. With only about 750 snow leopards left in the world, these animals are threatened with extinction.

Speedy runners

The great runners of the animal world have long, thin, muscular legs. Their feet are designed for the flat ground of plains, prairies, and deserts. Some run on four feet. Others run on two feet. These animals may run to flee a predator or to pursue prey. Some are long-distance runners. Some are sprinters. These champions run spectacular races.

A master sprinter

The cheetah is the fastest animal on earth. It has a supple spine that stretches like an accordion! It also has powerful back and leg muscles and long claws that grip the ground. This graceful feline can reach a speed of 50 miles (80 km) per hour in just two seconds. It can reach a top speed of 70 miles (112 km) per hour!

cheetah

Cool running

The bearded dragon is about 24 inches (60 cm) long including its tail. This reptile runs between desert rocks and climbs trees. When threatened by an enemy, it stands up on its hind legs, and using its long tail for balance, it dashes away. The lizard also runs like this to stay cool in hot weather.

bearded dragon

greater roadrunner

The American desert roadrunner

The greater roadrunner is the most famous running bird of all. It barely makes contact with the ground as it runs. It can reach a speed of 25 miles (40 km) per hour! The roadrunner rarely uses its short wings to fly, but they are helpful when it runs. The wings and the tail help the bird keep its balance during its wild runs through the desert.

Przewalski's horse

Running on hoof tips

Przewalski's horse is the last of the true wild horses, and only a few now live outside captivity. This horse is famous for its gallop. It runs on the tips of its hooves. Each hoof is an oversized, sturdy nail. Its long feet and muscular body also help make it one of the best runners in the animal world.

Are you curious?

The cheetah is a champion starter and short-distance sprinter, but after chasing prey for barely 20 seconds, it has used up so much energy that it has to stop for a rest. That's why its stomach remains empty three-quarters of the time.

Skilled explorers

Flatworms, earthworms, snails, leeches, and snakes know every inch of the ground by heart. They have no feet, but that's no problem! These expert explorers move around by simple contractions of their bodies. They slide and crawl on the Earth's surface. They slip into its deepest layers. They explore even the tiniest crevices. Every part of their bodies is in constant contact with the ground.

An undulating snake

The black mamba is 10 feet (3 m) long. It is the fastest snake in the world! It moves by an undulating (wavy) motion. Its body moves up and down and side to side between plant stems and stones. This snake can move at more than 12 miles (20 km) per hour.

black mamba

As slow as a snail

This snail secretes mucus that sticks to the ground under its foot. That helps the snail stay in one place. When the snail moves, a wave of contractions runs through its body. The mucus then becomes liquid and allows the animal to glide slowly over the ground.

five-banded snail

Nature's plows

Earthworms help keep soil healthy. They create air tunnels by swallowing earth as they move around. The earthworm crawls at a speed of about 12 inches (30 cm) per minute. It uses special muscles to move. The muscles allow the earthworm to lengthen and then shorten the sections of its body.

earthworm

Moving like an accordion

The European leech is about 4 inches (10 cm) long. At each tip of its body, the leech has a sucker. To move, it attaches the rear sucker to the ground. Then it stretches the front of its body like an accordion. Its body stretches to twice its original length. It then attaches its front sucker farther ahead, and, its rear sucker moves up to the front one. The leech keeps this up until it gets to where it is going.

medical leech

Are you curious?

When they undulate, snakes use plants, stones, and rough ground as supports. This helps them move fast without rolling over onto their backs.

Long-distance travelers

Millions of animals take long trips called migrations. They go by sea, by land, or by air. The trips range from a few miles (km) to thousands of miles (km). These animals migrate because of climate changes, food shortages, or the need to reproduce. The routes have many obstacles. Some long-distance travelers rely on their hearing, sense of smell, or vision. Others are guided by the earth's magnetic field or the position of the sun and stars.

A great traveler

The blue wildebeest, which is also called a gnu, lives in Tanzania. Every year, it begins a migration of more than 900 miles (1,500 km). Herds of these animals travel in search of water and fresh pastures. During this dangerous journey, several animals die. Some are trampled to death; some drown; and others become food for hyenas or lions.

blue wildebeest

Crisscrossing North America

In summer, monarch butterflies feed in groups in Canada and the northern United States. Their colorful wings create a lovely show. In autumn, they return to their winter homes in California, Mexico, and Florida. In spring, a new population of monarchs heads back north. Monarchs can fly up to 2,000 miles (3,200 km) without stopping for food, water, or rest!

monarch butterfly

Journey to the ends of the earth

In the animal world, the Arctic tern holds the distance record for migrations. This great traveler is about 17 inches (43 cm) long. It leaves its breeding grounds in the Arctic seas each August. Then it begins a migration of 22,000 miles (35,000 km) to the Antarctic ice pack! This amazing journey allows the tern to enjoy the best of both Poles.

Arctic tern

The trip of a lifetime

Few fish have a life as busy as that of the European eel. On the day of their birth, the tiny larvae begin a long and tiring journey. They swim 3,700 miles (6,000 km) from the salty waters of the Atlantic to the fresh waters of distant rivers. Twenty years later, they reach adulthood. Then they return to the warm waters to reproduce where they were born.

European eel

Are you curious?

Groups of females called harems are part of wildebeest societies. The harem of a single male may include as many as 150 females. The male protects the females against other males and against predators.

Non-movers

Not all animals can move. Some of them lead stationary lives. These creatures are completely immobile. They are born, grow old, and die in exactly the same place. To make up for being immobile, most of them have adapted in amazing ways.

A stationary colony

Corals live in groups called colonies. They build reefs in tropical seas. They have rigid limestone bodies attached to the skeletons of the corals that lived before them. Corals have a special way of feeding. Their stinging cells paralyze and capture any food that comes near. Corals also use food made by algae.

coral

A stationary life

After hatching, the female scale insect larva looks for a place to settle. It runs up and down the stem of the plant on which it is born. When it finds the right spot, it attaches itself and goes through an amazing change. Now it has no legs, wings, or eyes, and only tiny antennae. Scale insects spend their lives attached to the same plant and feed on its sap.

scale insect

fanworm

A flowery worm

Here is one flowery creature you should not pick! The beautiful plume of a fanworm is not a plant. This worm lives inside a rigid tube attached to the ocean floor. The fanworm attracts food toward its mouth by fluttering the millions of cilia (tiny hairs) on its tentacles.

A sedentary crustacean

The barnacle spends all of its adult life in the same position. The goose barnacle attaches itself to a floating object — a piece of wood, a buoy, or a bottle. This allows it to travel very long distances! The barnacle uses its bristly legs to get food. These unusual legs filter tiny plants and animals out of the seawater.

common goose barnacle

Are you curious?

The word "coral" comes from the Greek word korallion. It means "sea shrub." Since ancient times, these underwater animals have been "harvested." They are used to make jewelry and ornaments. Sometimes they are used to prepare potions with magical properties.

A map of where they live

More fun facts

GREAT ANIMAL PERFORMANCES		
	Running champions	**...and their speed (miles/km per hour)**
	Cheetah	70/112
	Springbok antelope	50/80
	Red deer	48/78
	Domestic horse	43/70
	Emu	40/64
	Ostrich	40/64
	Greyhound	37/60
	Lion	35/56
	Black rhinoceros	32/51
	Giraffe	32/51
	Timber wolf	28/45
	Grey monitor	14/22.5
	Black mamba	12/20
	Flying aces	**...and their speed (miles/km per hour)**
In a straight line	Peregrine falcon	112/180
	White-throated needletail	106/170
	Homing pigeon	94/151
	Spur-winged goose	88/142
	Green-winged teal	75/120
	Hawk	68/110
	Tundra swan	66/107
	Eurasian oystercatcher	62/100
	Whooper swan	58/93
	Willow ptarmigan	56/90
	Dragonfly	47/75
In a nosedive	Peregrine falcon	200/322
	Golden eagle	186/300
	Great swimmers	**...and their speed (miles/km per hour)**
	Swordfish	68/110
	Marlin	50/80
	Blue shark	43/70
	Bluefin tuna	43/70
	Killer whale	40/64
	Common dolphin	37/60
	Fin whale	30/48
	California sea lion	25/40
	Gentoo penguin	25/40
	Leatherback turtle	22/35

	Great jumpers	...and their performances (miles/km per hour)
High-jumpers	Mackerel shark	4.7/7.6
	Dolphin	4.3/7
	Killer whale	3.7/6
	Leopard	3.4/5.5
	Ibex	2.8/4.5
	Giant kangaroo	2.5/4
	Tiger	2.5/4
	Chamois	2.2/3.6
	Atlantic salmon	2.2/3.5
	Domestic dog	2.2/3.5
	Impala	1.9/3
	Domestic horse	1.52.5
Long-jumpers	Snow leopard	9/15
	Springbok antelope	9/15
	Giant kangaroo	8/13.5
	White-tailed deer	7.6/12.2
	Impala	7.6/12
	Domestic horse	7.4/11.9
	Killer whale	6.2/10
	Domestic dog	5.6/9
	Springhare	5.6/9
	Chamois	4.8/7.7
	Giant squirrel	3.7/6
	Frog	3.1/5
	Grasshopper	1.9/3
	Flea	0.2/0.33

	Skillful divers	...and their performances (feet/m)
	Sperm whale	9,843/3,000
	Sea elephant	4,101/1,250
	Baird's beaked whale	2,953/900
	Weddell seal	1,969/600
	Fin whale	1,640/500
	Emperor penguin	869/265
	Adelie penguin	230/70
	Diver	34/55

	World-class slowpokes	...and their speed
	Dwarf sea horse	62 hours to cover 1.6 miles (1 km)
	Brown snail	25 hours to cover 1.6 miles (1 km)
	Three-toed sloth	24 hours to cover 1.6 miles (km)
	Galapagos tortoise	3 hours to cover 1.6 miles (1 km)

For your information

hippopotamus

size	12 to 15 feet (3.7 to 4.6 m) long; 5 feet (1.4 m) tall
weight	about 3,000 pounds (1,361 kg)
distribution	sub-Saharan Africa
habitat	lakes, rivers
diet	grasses
reproduction	1 baby; 24-day gestation period
predators	humans, lions
life span	45 years (in captivity)

class Mammals
order Artiodactylae
family Hippopotamidae

Atlantic spotted dolphin

size	6 to 8 feet (1.8 to 2.4 m)
weight	243 to 320 pounds (110 to 145 kg)
distribution	Atlantic Ocean, tropical and temperate zones of the Gulf of Mexico
habitat	coastal regions
diet	fish, cephalopods
reproduction	1 baby; 11-month gestation period

class Mammals
order Cetacea
family Delphinidae

pearly nautilus

size	6 to 8 inches (15 to 20 cm) long
distribution	Indian and Pacific Oceans
habitat	depths of 164 to 328 feet (50 to 100 m)
diet	crustaceans, fish

class Cephalopods
order Tetrabranchiata
family Nautilidae

African jaçana

size	8.5 to 11 inches (22 to 28 cm)
distribution	sub-Saharan Africa
habitat	lakes, rivers, swamps, slow-moving waterways
diet	insects, mollusks, small fish, seeds
reproduction	4 to 6 eggs (up to four clutches per season); 22- to 24-day incubation period

class Birds
order Charadriiformes
family Jacanidae

tokay gecko

size	11 to 14 inches (28 to 35 cm)
distribution	India, Pakistan, southern China, Indochina, Philippines and Indonesia
habitat	trees, rocks, human dwellings
diet	spiders, insects, small lizards and young rodents
reproduction	1 to 2 eggs (4 to 6 clutches per year); 120- to 140-day incubation period

class Reptiles
order Squamata
family Gekkonidae

wandering albatross

size	3.3 feet (1 m) long; wingspan: 10 to 11 feet (3 to 3.5 m)
distribution	Antarctic islands and the coastal regions of the southern continents
habitat	ocean
diet	cephalopods, fish, crustaceans, and refuse from ships
reproduction	1 to 2 eggs every 2 years; 70- to 80-day incubation period
life span	30 years

class Birds
order Procellariiformes
family Diomedeidae

Malayan flying lemur

size	13 to 16 inches (33 to 42 cm) long;
weight	2.2 to 3.9 pounds (1 to 1.75 kg)
distribution	southeastern Asia, from Burma to Borneo
habitat	forests, plantations, plains
diet	shoots, buds, flowers, fruit, leaves
reproduction	1 baby; 60-day gestation period
predators	Philippine eagle, humans
life span	unknown

class Mammals
order Dermoptera
family Cynocephalidae

snow leopard

size	3.3 to 5 feet (1 to 1.5 m) long;
weight	55 to 155 pounds (25 to 70 kg)
distribution	Pakistan, from northern Afghanistan to Siberia, east of the Himalayas as far as China
habitat	alpine prairies, mountain slopes, forests
diet	hares, wild boars, sheep, goats , birds
reproduction	2 to 5 young; 90- to 103-day gestation period
life span	16 to 18 years (in captivity)

class Mammals
order Carnivora
family Felidae

cheetah

size	5 to 7 feet (1.5 to 2 m) long with tail; 2.3 to 3 feet (0.7 to 0 .9 m) tall
weight	77 to 155 pounds (35 to 70 kg)
distribution	Africa
habitat	semi-desert, steppes, and savannahs
diet	hares, jackals, gazelles, wildebeests, birds, zebras
reproduction	1 to 8 young; 90- to 95-day gestation period
predators	lions, panthers, hyenas, African hunting dogs
life span	20 years (in captivity)

class Mammals
order Carnivora
family Felidae

black mamba

size	10 feet (3 m) long
distribution	Africa from Senegal in the west to Kenya in the east and as far as southern Africa
habitat	savannahs and dry tropical forests
diet	birds and small mammals
reproduction	9 to 14 eggs
predators	eagles

class Reptiles
order Squamata
family Elapidae

blue wildebeest

size	7.5 to 11 feet (2.3 to 3.4 m) long with tail
weight	310 to 575 pounds (140 to 260 kg)
distribution	eastern and southern Africa
habitat	savannahs, steppes, sparse forests
diet	young grass shoots
reproduction	1 baby; 8- to 9-month gestation period
predators	lions, spotted hyenas, leopards, cheetahs, crocodiles, jackals, African hunting dogs
life span	18 to 20 years

class Mammals
order Artiodactylae
family Bovidae

coral

distribution	all seas and oceans, especially warm, shallow tropical seas
habitat	tropical, temperate, and even cold waters
diet	aquatic larvae, fish eggs, tiny crustaceans, little worms
predators	parrotfish, marine gastropods, worms, crustaceans, boxfish, lionfish

class Anthozoans
order 7 different orders of coral

Glossary

bristle: A short, stiff hair

cephalopod: Any of a class of mollusks that includes the octopus and the squid

colony: A group of beings living together

contraction: The shortening of a muscle

crevice: A narrow split or crack

crustacean: Any of a class of animals that have shells and many pairs of legs

current: Air or water that moves in a certain direction

dense: Having a high mass per unit volume

dorsal: Located on or near the back

Earth's magnetic field: The area on the Earth's surface that is magnetized by the North Pole

extinct: No longer existing

hover: To hang fluttering in the air

immobile: Not moving

larva: An often wormlike form that is one stage of an animal's life

limestone: Rock made up mainly of calcium carbonate

mammal: A member of any animal species in which the female has mammary glands for feeding her young

mangrove: A tropical tree or shrub that rests on roots growing above the ground

membrane: A thin layer of living cells

millipede: A wormlike animal with a segmented body and many legs

mollusk: An animal with a soft body that has no bones but usually has a hard shell

mucus: Transparent, viscous liquid

obstacle: Something that gets in the way of progress

predator: An animal that destroys or eats another

prehensile: Capable of grasping and picking things up

prey: An animal that is the victim of a predator

reptile: A crawling animal with scale-covered skin, such as the snake, the iguana, and the tortoise

rigid: Stiff and unyeilding

rodent: A mammal such as a mouse or a hamster with front teeth made for gnawing

sedentary: Sitting, not moving

siphon: A tube that sucks in water or allows it to circulate

spiral: Rolled in the shape of a winding curve that moves further away from a fixed point with each turn

sprinter: A runner who specializes in reaching and maintaining top speed over short distances

stationary: Immobile, not moving

streamlined: Shaped to offer minimum resistance; often tapered at both ends like a rocket

sucker: An organ in some animals that holds it to a surface

supple: Able to bend or twist easily and gracefully

tropical: Relating to or occurring in a frost-free climate with warm temperatures

tube foot: A tube-shaped outgrowth that has suckers

undulation: The movement of something that rises and falls, like waves

valve: A flaplike structure that opens and closes to control the flow of fluid

venom: The poison that is secreted by animals such as snakes

webbed: Having fingers or toes connected by a membrane

wingspan: The distance between the tips of spread or open wings

Index

32

Editorial Director Caroline Fortin **Research and Editing** Martine Podesto **Documentation** Anne-Marie Brault, Anne-Marie Labrecque, Jessie Daigle
Page Setup Lucie Mc Brearty **Illustrations** François Escalmel, Jocelyn Gardner **Translator** Gordon Martin **Copy Editing** Veronica Schami
Gareth Stevens editing Joan Downing **Cover Design** Joel Bucaro, Scott Krall